YOU KNOW YOU ARE

A DOG LOVER...

by Richard McChesney

illustrated by Rupert Besley

You Know You Are A Dog Lover... shows man's best friend right where he or she belongs – in charge!

This is the fourth book in the "You Know You Are" book series, and was compiled with help from dogs and their owners for you to love and laugh together.

Other books in the "You Know You Are" series are:

- You Know You Are A Runner...
- You Know You Are A Nurse...
- You Know You Are An Engineer...
- You Know You Are A Golfer...
- You Know You Are Getting Older...
- You Know You Are A Teacher...
- You Know You Are A Mother...

Visit www.YouKnowYouAreBooks.com to join our mailing list and be notified when future titles are released, or find us at www.facebook.com/YouKnowYouAreBooks, or follow us on twitter (@YouKnowYouAreBK)

Happy reading!

YOU KNOW YOU ARE A DOG LOVER
WHEN YOU KNOW ALL THE DOGS
IN THE NEIGHBORHOOD BY NAME
BUT NOT THEIR OWNERS...

YOU KNOW YOU ARE A DOG LOVER
WHEN YOU THINK EVERYONE APPRECIATES
A GOOD DOGGY KISS...

YOU KNOW YOU ARE A DOG LOVER
WHEN YOUR DOG EATS BETTER THAN YOU DO...

YOU KNOW YOU ARE A DOG LOVER
WHEN YOU ONLY GO TO PLACES
WHERE YOUR DOG IS WELCOME...

YOU KNOW YOU ARE A DOG LOVER
WHEN YOU SPEND MORE ON YOUR DOG'S
GROOMING THAN ON YOUR OWN...

YOU KNOW YOU ARE A DOG LOVER
WHEN YOUR DOG HAS MORE TOYS THAN YOUR CHILDREN...

YOU KNOW YOU ARE A DOG LOVER
WHEN YOUR VACATION PHOTOS ARE MORE
DOGS THAN SCENERY...

YOU KNOW YOU ARE A DOG LOVER
WHEN YOUR DOGS HAVE MORE PRESENTS UNDER THE CHRISTMAS TREE THAN YOU DO...

YOU KNOW YOU ARE A DOG LOVER
WHEN YOU BUY ANOTHER SOFA TO REPLACE
THE ONE EATEN BY YOUR PUPPY...

YOU KNOW YOU ARE A DOG LOVER
WHEN THE UMBRELLA IS NOT FOR
YOU BUT FOR YOUR DOG...

YOU KNOW YOU ARE A DOG LOVER
WHEN YOU DON'T THINK TWICE ABOUT
TRADING LICKS OF AN ICE-CREAM
WITH YOUR DOG...

YOU KNOW YOU ARE A DOG LOVER
WHEN YOUR WORK DESK HAS PHOTOS OF
YOUR DOGS, BUT NONE OF YOUR FAMILY...

YOU KNOW YOU ARE A DOG LOVER
WHEN YOUR KING-SIZE BED IS
STILL TOO SMALL...

YOU KNOW YOU ARE A DOG LOVER
WHEN YOUR DOG HAS ON AT LEAST ONE
ITEM OF YOUR CLOTHING...

YOU KNOW YOU ARE A DOG LOVER

WHEN YOUR BACK YARD HAS 8 TENNIS
BALLS AND 3 FRISBEES HIDDEN
AMONGST THE PLANTS...

YOU KNOW YOU ARE A DOG LOVER
WHEN YOU EXPLAIN COMPLEX
SITUATIONS TO YOUR DOG,
JUST IN CASE HE UNDERSTANDS...

YOU KNOW YOU ARE A DOG LOVER
WHEN YOU AND YOUR DOG HAVE GAZED
LOVINGLY INTO EACH OTHER'S EYES...

YOU KNOW YOU ARE A DOG LOVER
WHEN YOU LEAVE SOCIAL EVENTS EARLY TO 'GO HOME AND FEED THE DOG'...

YOU KNOW YOU ARE A DOG LOVER
WHEN YOU COME BACK FROM VACATION
WITH GIFTS FOR YOUR DOG...

YOU KNOW YOU ARE A DOG LOVER
WHEN STEPPING BAREFOOT ROUND
THE HOUSE MEANS STUBBING
YOUR TOES ON DOG BONES ...

YOU KNOW YOU ARE A DOG LOVER
WHEN YOU HOARD PLASTIC BAGS,
BECAUSE THEY DO HAVE THEIR USES...

YOU KNOW YOU ARE A DOG LOVER
WHEN YOU BELIEVE THE SMELL OF
YOUR DOG'S BREATH IS LIKE A
SWEET SCENTED PERFUME...

YOU KNOW YOU ARE A DOG LOVER
WHEN YOU START TELLING YOUR KIDS TO 'SIT', 'STAY' AND 'LEAVE IT'...

YOU KNOW YOU ARE A DOG LOVER
WHEN YOU TAKE DOGS WITH YOU WHEN
TEST DRIVING A NEW CAR...

YOU KNOW YOU ARE A DOG LOVER
WHEN YOUR SWEATSHIRT IS MISTAKEN
FOR A FABULOUS ANGORA...

YOU KNOW YOU ARE A DOG LOVER
WHEN YOU'VE USED THE EXCUSE
'MY DOG ATE MY HOMEWORK'
AND IT'S ACTUALLY TRUE...

YOU KNOW YOU ARE A DOG LOVER
WHEN YOU CAN'T SEE OUT OF THE CAR FOR NOSE-PRINTS ON THE WINDSCREEN...

YOU KNOW YOU ARE A DOG LOVER
WHEN YOUR DOG HAS HIS OWN FACEBOOK PAGE...

YOU KNOW YOU ARE A DOG LOVER
WHEN YOUR GUESTS ARE INTRODUCED TO THE DOG BEFORE THEY EVEN ENTER...

YOU KNOW YOU ARE A DOG LOVER
WHEN CARPET CLEANER AND PAPER
TOWELS ARE AT THE TOP OF YOUR
WEEKLY SHOPPING LIST...

YOU KNOW YOU ARE A DOG LOVER
WHEN YOU ALWAYS CARRY EXTRA
DOG BISCUITS, JUST IN CASE...

YOU KNOW YOU ARE A DOG LOVER
WHEN YOU KNOW EXACTLY WHAT YOUR DOG
IS SAYING BY THE BARK SHE IS USING...

YOU KNOW YOU ARE A DOG LOVER
WHEN YOUR CHOICE OF NEW HOUSE IS
DECIDED ON KENNEL-SPACE...

YOU KNOW YOU ARE A DOG LOVER
WHEN ALL THAT MATTERS IS
FIRST PRIZE IN THE DOG SHOW...

YOU KNOW YOU ARE A DOG LOVER
WHEN YOUR PERFECT TREAT OUT IS
A SEAT AT A DOG SHOW...

YOU KNOW YOU ARE A DOG LOVER
WHEN YOUR DOG DECIDES HE DOESN'T LIKE SOMEONE AND YOU TEND TO AGREE...

YOU KNOW YOU ARE A DOG LOVER
WHEN YOU'VE TRACED YOUR DOG'S FAMILY
TREE BACK FURTHER THAN YOUR OWN...

YOU KNOW YOU ARE A DOG LOVER
WHEN YOUR DOG INHERITS ALL
YOUR WORLDLY GOODS...

So... are you a Dog Lover?

You have just read the fourth book in the "You Know You Are" series.

Other "You Know You Are" books are:

- You Know You Are A Runner...
- You Know You Are A Nurse...
- You Know You Are An Engineer...
- You Know You Are A Golfer...
- You Know You Are Getting Older...
- You Know You Are A Teacher...
- You Know You Are A Mother...

If you enjoyed this book why not join our mailing list to be notified when future titles are released – visit www.YouKnowYouAreBooks.com, or find us on facebook (www.facebook.com/YouKnowYouAreBooks), or follow us on twitter (@YouKnowYouAreBK)